OPPOSITES

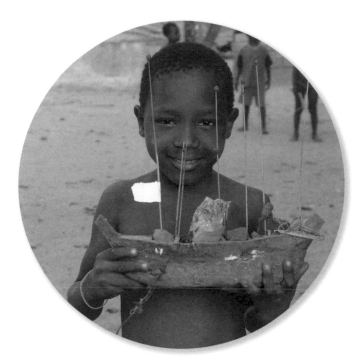

Kathy Knowles

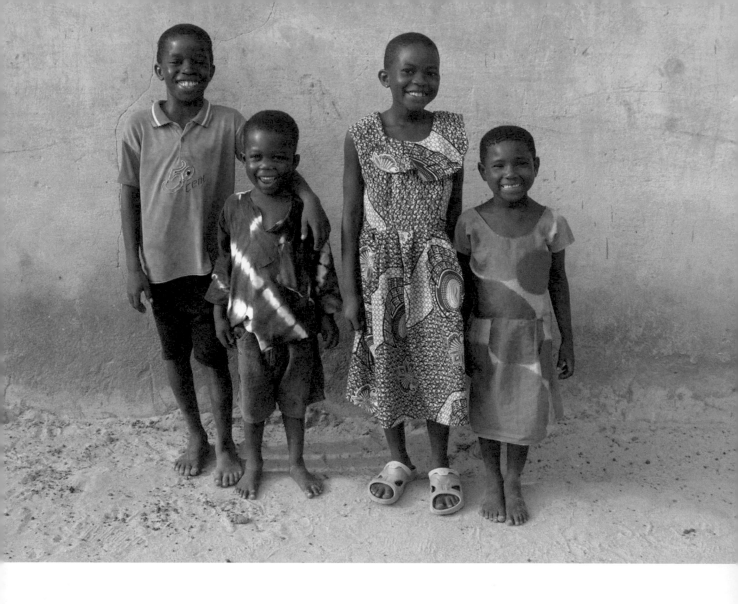

Let's learn about opposites!

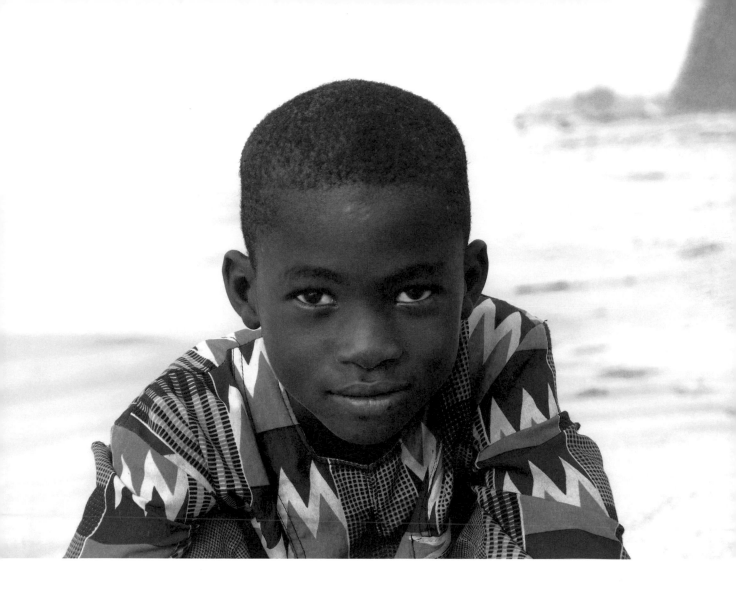

What is the opposite of front?

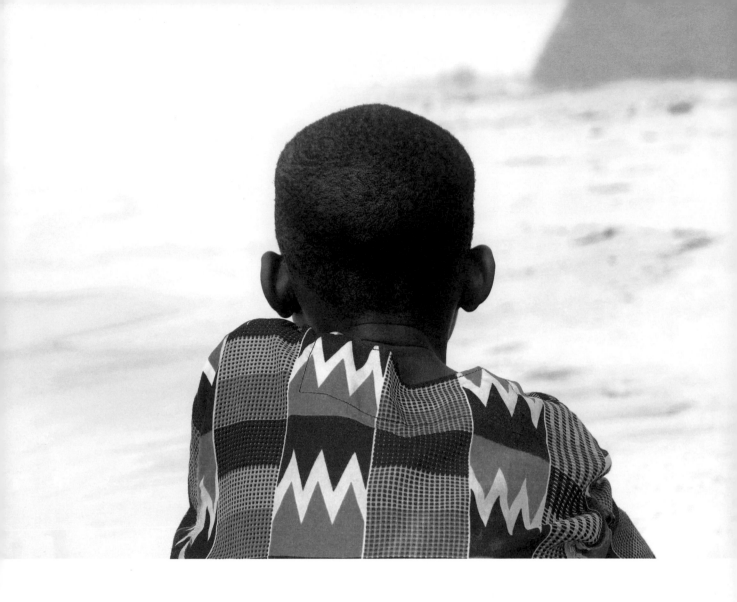

Back.

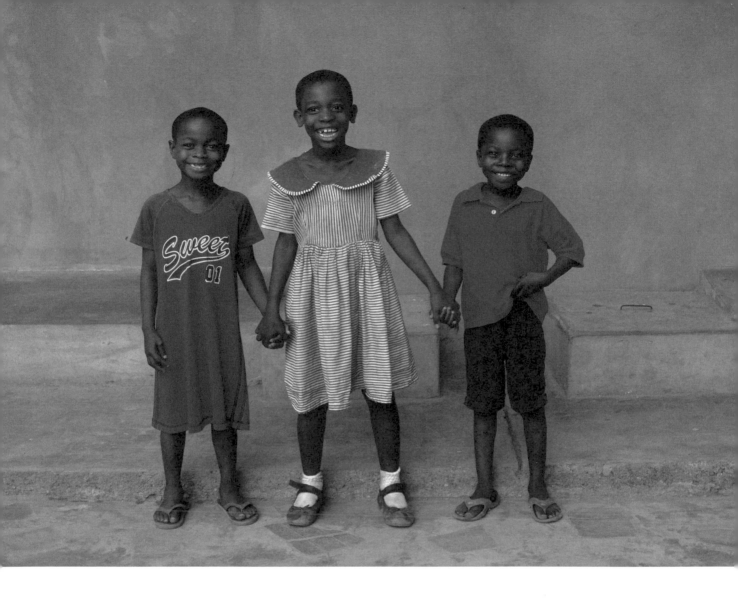

What is the opposite of together?

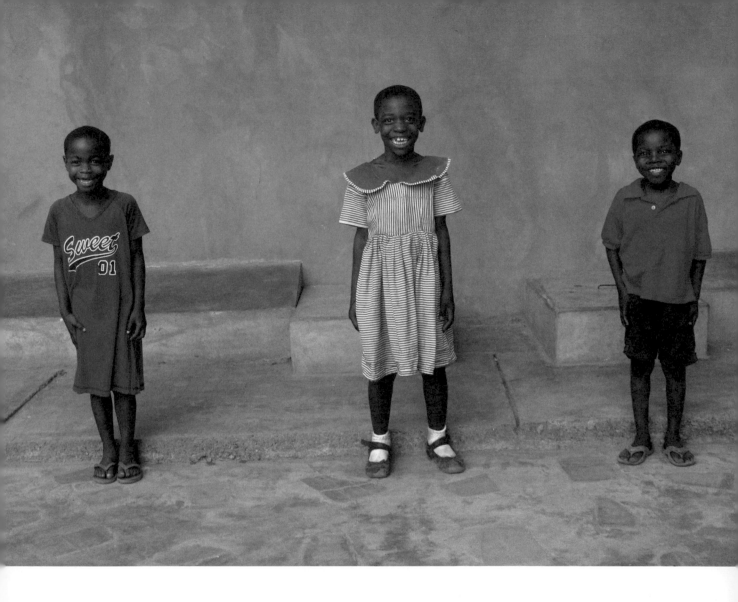

Apart.

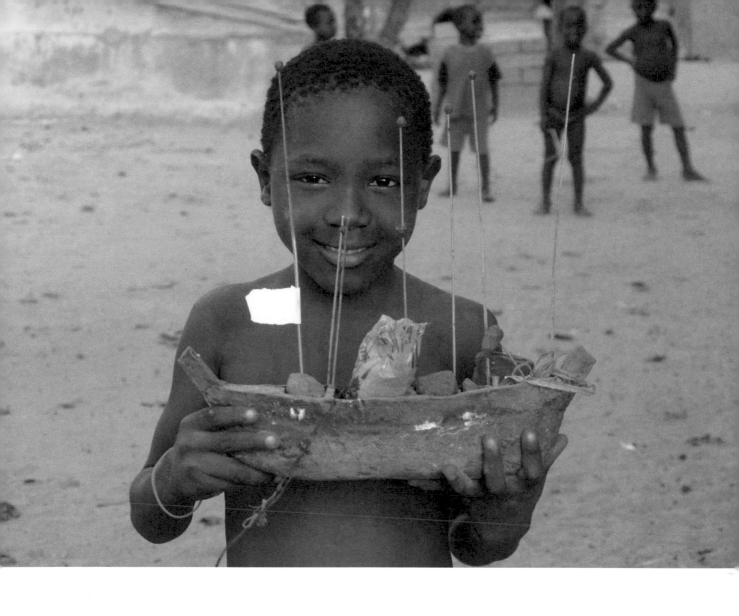

What is the opposite of little?

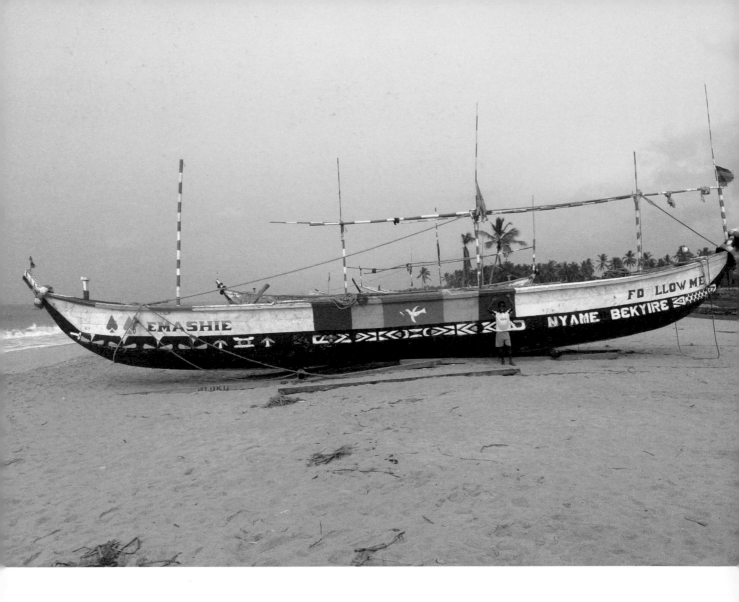

Big.

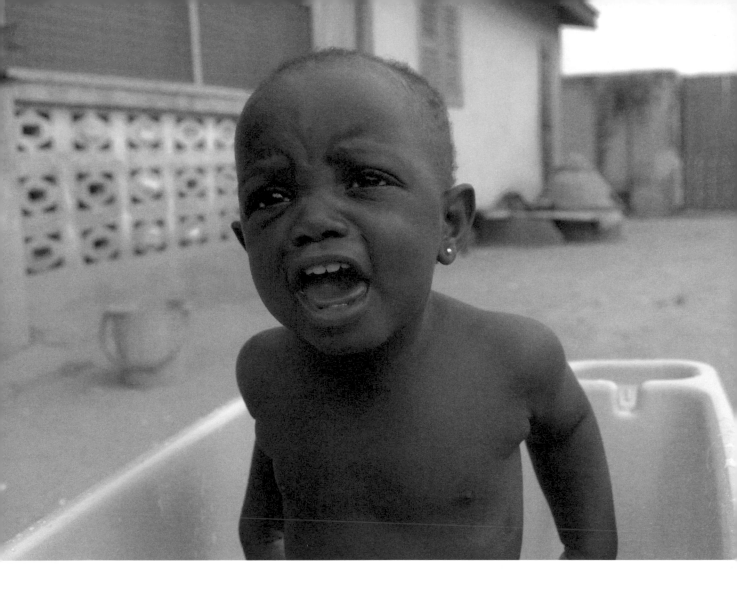

What is the opposite of sad?

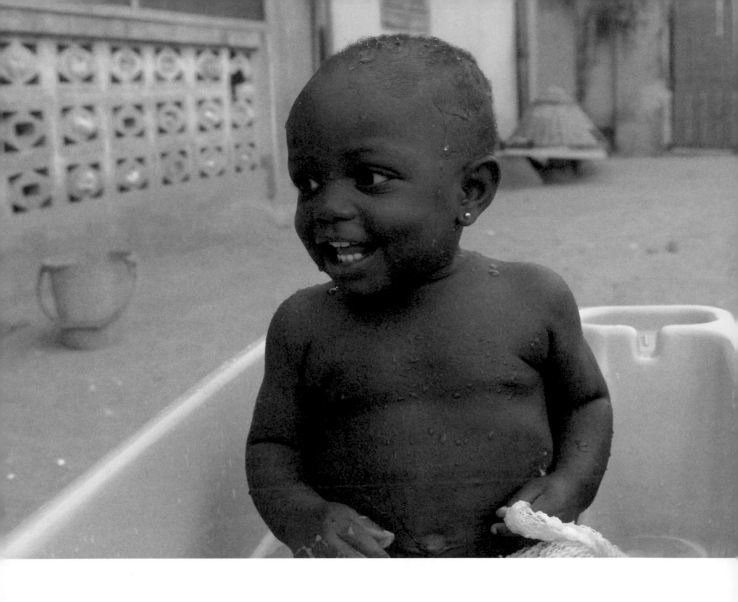

Happy.

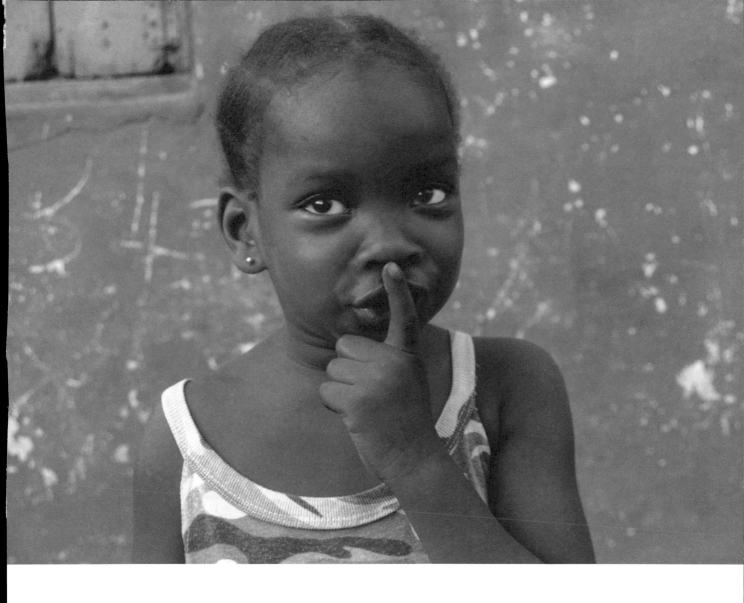

What is the opposite of quiet?

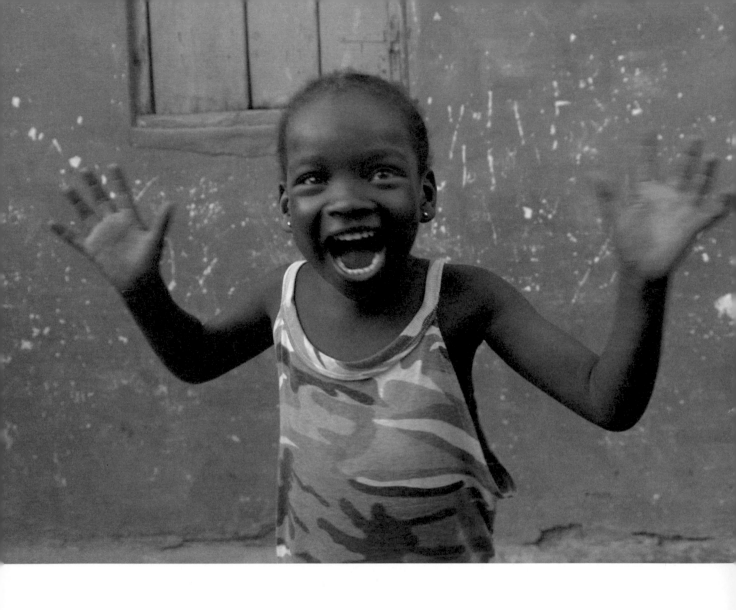

Loud!